Loans
not
at th
3 ti
P'

24.

History *of* Britain
Roman Villas
and Great Houses

Brenda Williams

Illustrated by Mark Bergin

HISTORY OF BRITAIN – ROMAN VILLAS AND GREAT HOUSES
was produced for Heinemann Children's Reference
by Lionheart Books, London.

Editors: Lionel Bender, Sue Reid
Designer: Ben White
Editorial Assistant: Madeleine Samuel
Picture Researcher: Jennie Karrach
Media Conversion and Typesetting: Peter MacDonald

Educational Consultant: Jane Shuter
Editorial Advisors: Andrew Farrow, Paul Shuter

Production Controller: Lorraine Stebbing
Editorial Director: David Riley

First published in Great Britain in 1997 by
Heinemann Educational Publishers, a division of Reed
Educational and Professional Publishing Limited,
Halley Court, Jordan Hill, Oxford OX2 8EJ.

MADRID ATHENS
FLORENCE PRAGUE WARSAW
PORTSMOUTH NH CHICAGO SAO PAULO MEXICO
SINGAPORE TOKYO MELBOURNE AUCKLAND
IBADAN GABORONE JOHANNESBURG KAMPALA NAIROBI

© Reed Educational & Professional Publishing Ltd 1997

ISBN 0 431 05710 9 Hb   ISBN 0 431 05714 1 Pb

British Library Cataloguing-in-Publication Data.
A catalogue record for this book is available
from the British Library.

Printed in Italy

Acknowledgements
Picture Credits
t = top, b = bottom, l = left, r = right, c = centre.
Pages 5, 6t: Fishbourne Roman Palace/Sussex Archaeological Society.
6b: Scala Photo Library, Italy. 8t: Museum of London. 9: Museum of
London. 11tl: English Heritage Photographic Library. 11tr: Copyright
British Museum. 12cl: Verulamium Museum. 12tr, 13: C.M. Dixon.
14: Museum of London. 15tl: English Heritage Photographic Library.
15c: National Museums of Scotland. 16: English Heritage Photographic
Library. 17t: Hunting Aerofilms Ltd. 17b: Colchester Museums. 18: C.M.
Dixon. 19t: Lesley & Roy Adkins. 19cr: Michael Holford. 20: Ikona/The
Vatican Museum, Rome. 21: C.M. Dixon. 22tr: Ashmolean Museum,
Oxford. 22b: English Heritage Photographic Library.

All artwork by Mark Bergin except map on page 23, by Stefan Chabluk.

Cover: Artwork by Mark Bergin. Photos: Museum of London (Writing
tablet, stylus and ink pot), C. M. Dixon (late-Roman silver dish).

PLACES TO VISIT

Here are some Roman villas and other sites you can visit.
Your local tourist office will be able to tell you about places
in your area.

Bignor, West Sussex. Important villa site with mosaics.

Brading, Isle of Wight. Remains of villa and mosaics.

Chedworth, near Cirencester, Gloucestershire. One of the
best-preserved villas in Britain.

Ditchley, Oxfordshire. Second-century 'winged corridor' villa.

Fishbourne, near Chichester, West Sussex. Remains of the
largest building in Roman Britain, possibly the palace of
Cogidubnus.

Great Witcombe, Gloucestershire. Outstanding setting for
a villa. Remains include a corn-drier.

Llantwit Major, South Glamorgan, Wales. Remains of villa
and farm estate.

Lockleys, near Welwyn, Hertfordshire. Remains of farmer's
simple cottage-house.

London. British Museum and Museum of London; remains
of Roman city wall and Temple of Mithras, which was found
in 1954 near the Mansion House. Remains of the Roman
Governor's palace have been found but are now built over.

Lullingstone, Kent. Villa with impressive dining room.

North Leigh, Oxfordshire. Wall foundations and a mosaic
remain of a courtyard-style villa.

Rockbourne, Hampshire. Villa site with a museum.

St Albans, Hertfordshire. Walls, remains of Roman
Verulamium, including theatre, and remains of Celtic
settlement.

Silchester, Hampshire. Remains of Roman town.

Woodchester, Gloucestershire. Second-century villa noted
for its mosaic floor.

York, North Yorkshire. Yorkshire Museum has Roman
blacksmith's gravestone. City has remains of legionary
fortress, partly under the medieval cathedral.

INTRODUCTION

In AD 43, the Romans invaded southern Britain. They quickly made it part of their huge empire, which was centred on Rome in Italy. They built supply bases, forts, roads and towns. Wealthy Romans – and some Britons – began building country residences as well. As farmers sold grain to feed the Roman army, they grew richer. Many of them replaced their old thatched houses with new homes built in Roman style. Such houses in the countryside were known as villas. They varied from humble farm dwellings to country houses or luxurious mansions as grand as palaces. Most villas shared a similar style of building and were working farms that also served as comfortable family homes.

CONTENTS

BUILDING A VILLA

Villas were country homes, and usually parts of farming estates (areas of land). In Britain, most villas were built in the south, on fertile land in easy reach of town markets. Out of 600 villas found in Britain, 75 were particularly grand houses.

▽ **Building the Roman villa at Fishbourne in AD 75.** Red and yellow stone from the Mediterranean area and white marble from Italy were brought to Fishbourne by ship. Blue, grey and black stone for floors and walls came from British quarries. Carts delivered the building materials to the site by road.

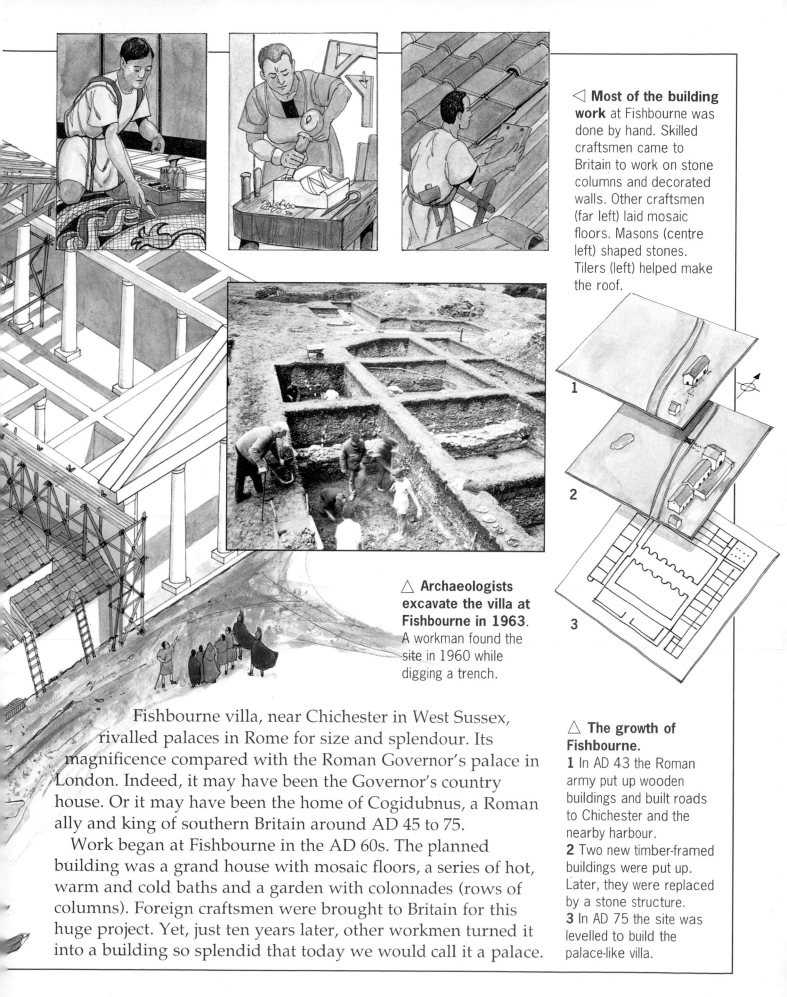

△ **Most of the building work** at Fishbourne was done by hand. Skilled craftsmen came to Britain to work on stone columns and decorated walls. Other craftsmen (far left) laid mosaic floors. Masons (centre left) shaped stones. Tilers (left) helped make the roof.

△ **Archaeologists excavate the villa at Fishbourne in 1963**. A workman found the site in 1960 while digging a trench.

△ **The growth of Fishbourne.**
1 In AD 43 the Roman army put up wooden buildings and built roads to Chichester and the nearby harbour.
2 Two new timber-framed buildings were put up. Later, they were replaced by a stone structure.
3 In AD 75 the site was levelled to build the palace-like villa.

Fishbourne villa, near Chichester in West Sussex, rivalled palaces in Rome for size and splendour. Its magnificence compared with the Roman Governor's palace in London. Indeed, it may have been the Governor's country house. Or it may have been the home of Cogidubnus, a Roman ally and king of southern Britain around AD 45 to 75.

Work began at Fishbourne in the AD 60s. The planned building was a grand house with mosaic floors, a series of hot, warm and cold baths and a garden with colonnades (rows of columns). Foreign craftsmen were brought to Britain for this huge project. Yet, just ten years later, other workmen turned it into a building so splendid that today we would call it a palace.

FIT FOR A KING

Rich Romans built villas that were far more comfortable and luxurious than any house seen in Britain for the next thousand years. Villa owners made improvements, such as adding hypocausts and mosaic floors, as and when they could afford them.

The palace of Fishbourne was built on four sides around a garden on a site covering about 2 hectares (the size of two soccer pitches). Tonnes of soil were carted away to level the ground for building. Changes were made to the palace over the years, until fire destroyed it at the end of the 3rd century.

The original palace had about 100 rooms, with a main courtyard about 60 metres square. Visitors arriving by road from Chichester were awed by the huge entrance hall in the centre of the east side. They walked up steps to a pool with fountains playing and into the high-roofed hall held up by huge columns. Visitors on official business went to the audience chamber along a wide, hedge-lined path.

Nearly all of the rooms had mosaic floors. These were some of the first in Britain, laid by craftsmen from Gaul (France) or Italy. Most rooms opened out on to columned verandas, letting light and air into the building. From the south side of the palace, people gazed out over a terraced garden. Beyond its stream, pond, fountains, shrubs and trees lay the sea. Boats were moored at the garden edge.

△ **In the gardens at Fishbourne,** excavations revealed the trenches dug by Roman gardeners alongside paths. Many Roman gardens had paths lined by hedges.

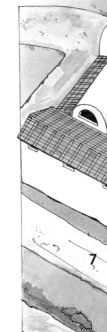

▽ **Wall paintings from Rome,** more than 1,500 years old, show views of a large Roman palace with a grand entrance, colonnades and gardens.

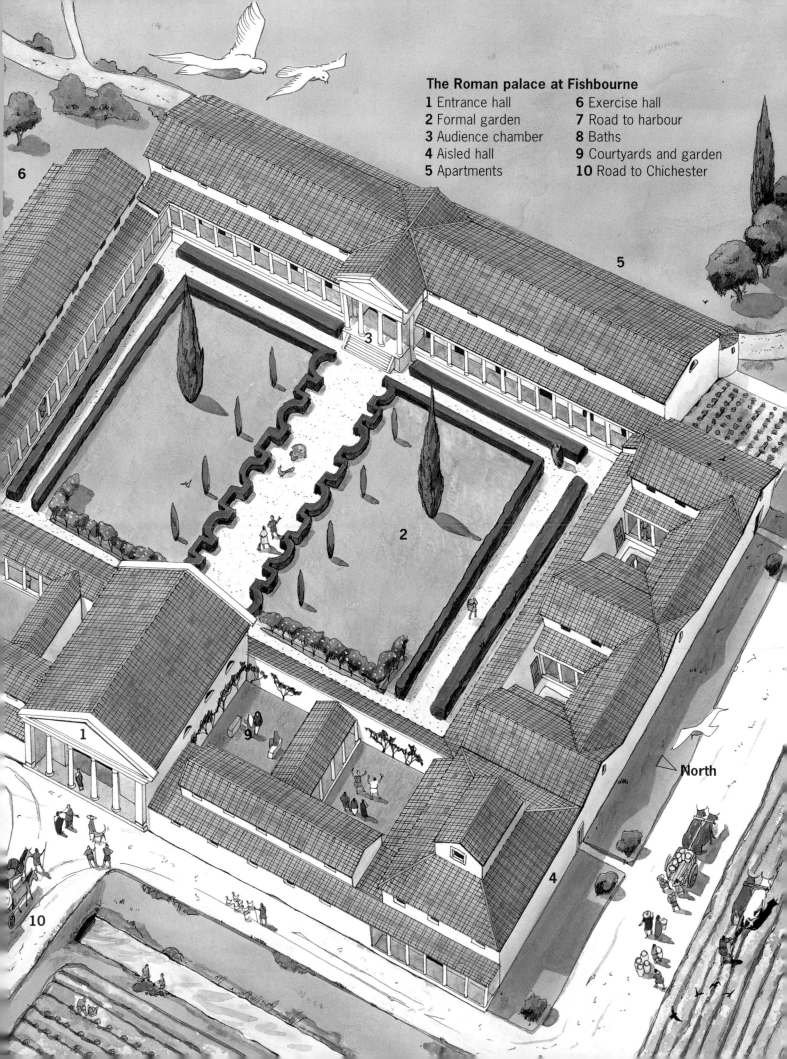

The Roman palace at Fishbourne

1 Entrance hall
2 Formal garden
3 Audience chamber
4 Aisled hall
5 Apartments
6 Exercise hall
7 Road to harbour
8 Baths
9 Courtyards and garden
10 Road to Chichester

North

RUNNING THE COUNTRY

Fishbourne was not the only Roman palace in Britain. The Governor's palace in London, built between about AD 85 and 100, was probably as large and as luxurious. From here, the whole of Britain was run and administered.

It was the job of the Governor of Britain to keep the province (known as Britannia) running smoothly. To do this, he needed a large staff at his London palace. Local officials dealt with local business, such as collecting taxes. Everyone in Britain had to pay taxes to the Roman government and obey the emperor.

△ **A 1st century seal box lid.** Government documents were tied with cord threaded through a small box with a seal inside.

△ **All these people lived and worked in the London palace.**
The Governor of Britain usually held the job for three to five years. He and his wife and children – shown above dressed in typical Roman clothes – would have lived and worked in other parts of the Roman Empire, too.

Government officials (above right) made sure that the Governor's orders were carried out. Officials included educated slaves and freedmen. Roman citizens had to obey Roman laws. Ordinary Britons kept their own laws. Officials in the Governor's finance office paid the army,

collected taxes and looked after the empire's mines and estates. Officials also organized the census (head count) to find out how many people should pay taxes. All officials kept careful records. These were written in pen and ink on papyrus or parchment rolls and stored on shelves or in cupboards.

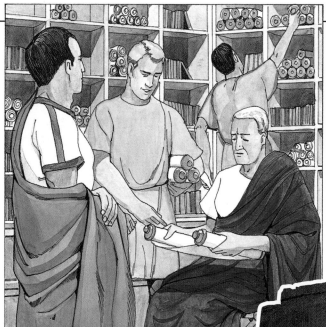

◁ **Large villa estates needed many people to run them.** To run both the province and his palace in London, the Governor of Britain had a staff of more than 200. As well as officials, the palace staff included clerks, grooms, soldiers, cleaners, prison guards, and executioners.

▽ **Records** were written on rolls or on waxed wooden tablets using a pointed stylus.

Stylus

Wooden writing tablet

△ **Army officers,** such as these two centurions in uniform, commanded the soldiers guarding the Governor's palace. They also protected government officials on duty in their travels round Britain.

All villa estates were run in a similar way. Villa owners were responsible for looking after their own lands. They also had to keep accurate records of what they owned, grew, bought and sold. Then the government worked out how much tax they must pay, in grain or money. A villa owner employed a secretary, clerks and scribes to keep the records. Many owners hired an overseer to run their farms or to be in charge if they lived in a town.

In Roman Britain, owning land was a mark of importance. The head of a landowning family could sit on a town council and stand for election as a magistrate. He then had a say in local business, building and law, and in how taxes were collected and spent. The Roman writer Tacitus says that Britons paid their taxes promptly. But not all tax collectors were fair. At least one container found for collecting corn held more grain than the measurements marked on the outside!

THE FAMILY HOUSE

Most villas, no matter how big or richly decorated, were intended to be family homes. Parents, children and relations all lived together. The servants who ran the house lived apart from the family.

Passages led from the villa's main reception room, or atrium, to the living quarters. Men's and women's rooms were often separate, although husbands and wives shared a room. Young children slept in the women's rooms.

Villas had a variety of rooms, including a library and study where family documents were kept. Lullingstone villa in Kent had few other rooms apart from its splendid dining room. This was unusual. Perhaps this villa was built for pleasure rather than as a working estate-owner's home.

Furniture in most villas was quite simple and made of wood, often by the estate carpenters. Only the very rich could afford elegant marble tables from Italy. Some beds were sprung with leather webbing, others had solid wooden bases. Rugs were laid on the floors.

Lavatories had wooden or stone seats over a sewer. People used sponges on sticks instead of toilet paper. The sponges were washed in a stream that flowed in a channel across the bathroom floor and into a nearby sewer.

▽ **The first British villas** were not as luxurious as grand homes in Italy. Homes had little furniture but walls were decorated with friezes and paintings.

▷ (Opposite) **Detail of a mosaic floor at Lullingstone villa.** The mosaic shows the capture of the Roman beauty, Europa, by the god Jupiter, disguised as a bull, with two cupids (winged boys) looking on.

10

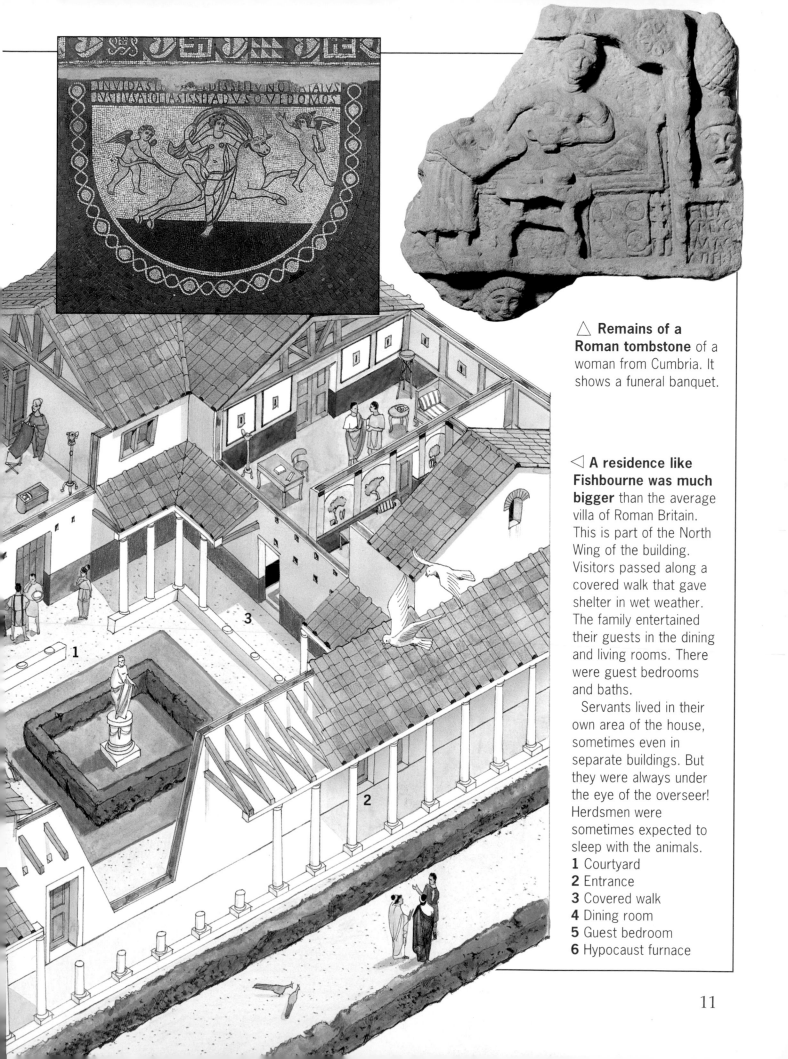

△ **Remains of a Roman tombstone** of a woman from Cumbria. It shows a funeral banquet.

◁ **A residence like Fishbourne was much bigger** than the average villa of Roman Britain. This is part of the North Wing of the building. Visitors passed along a covered walk that gave shelter in wet weather. The family entertained their guests in the dining and living rooms. There were guest bedrooms and baths.

Servants lived in their own area of the house, sometimes even in separate buildings. But they were always under the eye of the overseer! Herdsmen were sometimes expected to sleep with the animals.

1 Courtyard
2 Entrance
3 Covered walk
4 Dining room
5 Guest bedroom
6 Hypocaust furnace

RUNNING THE ESTATE

Running the villa and the lands around it was a year-round task. The villa's large staff of servants and slaves did the cooking and cleaning. Other labourers and slaves worked on the farm. Most of the villa's workers were bought or hired locally.

▽ **Pottery like this, dating from about AD 200, was often made on the estate.** Pollen that stuck to newly made pottery left to dry on the ground shows us which plants grew on villa farms. For special occasions, and as ornaments, a rich family could buy expensive pottery beakers and dishes made in Gaul or Italy.

▷ **A Roman tombstone from York shows a blacksmith** at his forge.

Members of the household included the family tutor and secretary as well as the personal servants and slaves who helped the family bathe and dress. Slaves belonged to the estate, like the farm animals. An overseer was in charge of running the estate. He gave orders to herdsmen and ploughmen, smiths, gardeners, carpenters and the men who stoked up the central heating furnaces. His wife was in charge of female slaves.

▽ **Cooks prepared food for the family and for banquets** when visitors came. Most of the food came from the estate farm and vegetable gardens. Surplus produce was sold in the market.

▽ **The hypocaust central heating system** kept the villa warm in winter. Slaves kept a wood fire burning in the furnace, sending hot air through a tile-lined channel under floors and up through walls.

▽ **Slaves made clothes for the family** and for themselves. Women spun wool from sheep and goats, and wove the yarn on hand looms into cloth. Vegetable dyes were used to colour the wool.

The villa had other workers, like potters and wagon drivers. On a large estate there would be a smith's forge (where bronze and iron tools were made), a mill (for grinding grain), and a slaughterhouse for butchering animals.

Villas that were the centres of busy farm estates had many outbuildings – cow sheds, barns, stables for horses, pig sties and sheepfolds. Grain was often threshed in the large farmyard. Damp corn was dried in hot-air kilns. Some villas even had a walled village on the estate.

Villa farms could be very large. Bignor villa in Sussex had about 800 hectares planted with crops.

Work began at daybreak. Fieldworkers went out to plough, sow seeds, pull weeds, or harvest crops. In winter, if the weather was too bad for outside work, slaves wove rush baskets or made fences for sheep pens, ready for the spring lambing.

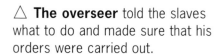

△ **The overseer** told the slaves what to do and made sure that his orders were carried out.

▽ **Carpenters** used iron planes (for smoothing wood), chisels and bow-drills. To measure, they used dividers, rulers, set squares and spirit levels.

△ **Shepherds** were used to the cool and wet British climate. They and the ploughmen and other labourers worked in all weathers.

△ (Above) **Bronze model of a ploughman and team of ox and cow**, from the Roman fort at Piercebridge, Durham.

13

FESTIVALS AND TEMPLES

Country people held festivals during the year to gain favour with the gods and goddesses who, they believed, kept crops growing and animals healthy. Every villa had its own household shrine for worship. Large villas had their own temples.

▽ **Mithras the Bull-slayer**, from the site of the Temple of Mithras, Walbrook, London, late 2nd or 3rd century AD. Only men were allowed to worship Mithras.

Many provinces of the Roman Empire had several different religions, which the Romans often took up and practised. But all Romans were also expected to celebrate the cult honouring the emperor. At festival times, the public temples were full of worshippers. In the country, little roadside shrines and temples were open to travellers and local people. Many country houses had their own temples.

△ **Bone disc** from Lullingstone, Kent, with the head of Medusa or a goddess. The disc was found on a coffin. Medusa's blood was thought to revive the dead.

◁ **Mithras, lord of light**, was a god popular among Roman soldiers. Worship of Mithras was introduced to the Roman Empire from Asia Minor by the army in the 1st century AD. Mithras stood for the qualities admired by soldiers – strength, courage and honesty.

◁ **This scene of a Roman temple** is based on the Temple of Mithras in London. The temple was a small building (7.9 metres wide and 17.8 metres long). The congregation entered through double doors and went down four steps to the wooden floor. They occupied wooden platforms in aisles either side of the central nave where rituals took place. Seven pairs of columns (only four pairs are seen here) supported the roof – a reminder of the seven grades through which worshippers of Mithras believed they must pass. There were sculptures of two attendant spirits and an altar at the front. Worshippers feasted in darkness, possibly sacrificing animals to the god (chicken bones have been found) and drinking magical potions of herbs.

△ **Detail of a Roman sculpture from Scotland** showing an altar (bottom left) and animals about to be sacrificed to the god Mars.

△ **A villa owner and his wife visiting the household shrine** where family ancestors were honoured and incense was burned.

Cogidubnus built a big temple on Hayling Island near his capital at Chichester. Owners of smaller villas kept statues of gods and goddesses in little shrines, or set up busts (carved stone figures of head and shoulders) of honoured ancestors. Several busts were found at Lullingstone villa. Other villas, like Chedworth, had garden shrines to which the family brought offerings of honey, wine or flowers to the gods.

Soldiers on duty at the Governor's palace went to the Temple of Mithras in Walbrook. Buildings probably used by Christians remain at Lullingstone, and Frampton villa in Dorset has mosaics with Christian designs. Other villa mosaics show Roman gods.

A DAY OF LEISURE

Some Romans took their pleasures seriously. The writer Cicero joked that "practically no one who is sober dances, unless he happens to be mad". Nevertheless, most people in Roman Britain enjoyed some sort of leisure activity or entertainment.

Rich families had lots of time for leisure. At home there were baths in which to relax, an exercise corridor for games, and gardens to walk in. Morning was the time for business; the afternoon was for leisure. There were plenty of holidays too: by about AD 350, the Romans had 175 days off work a year.

After lessons from the family tutor, children had time for their toys. They played with pull-along carts, animals made of bronze and pottery, wooden or rag dolls, and dolls' houses with furniture. For outdoor play, older children had hoops, tops, swings and see-saws. They played hide-and-seek and leap-frog. Grown-ups joined in ball games in the courtyard, unless the men had gone off hunting deer, boar or bears.

▷ **Relaxing at home in the villa.** The owner's wife plays with her son while slaves bring a snack meal and drinks. Gambling was popular, and the men shown here are exchanging the winnings from a bet.

▽ **A Roman gaming board, with counters and dice**. Dice-throwing was a popular indoor game.

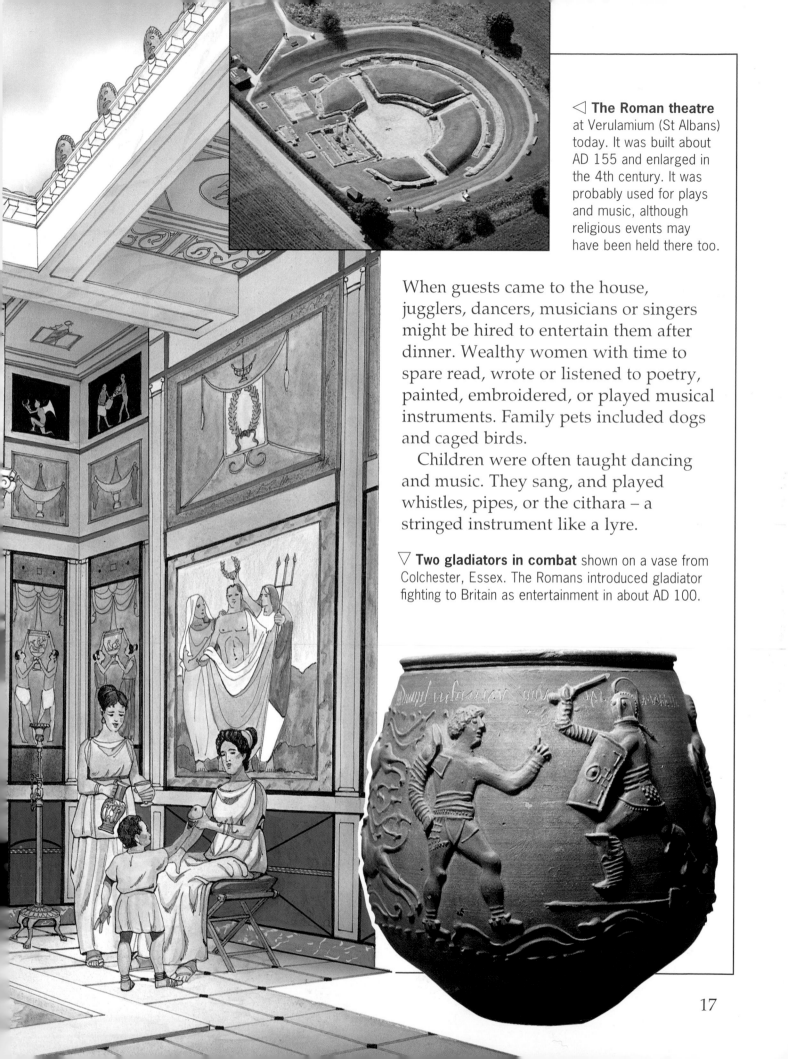

◁ **The Roman theatre** at Verulamium (St Albans) today. It was built about AD 155 and enlarged in the 4th century. It was probably used for plays and music, although religious events may have been held there too.

When guests came to the house, jugglers, dancers, musicians or singers might be hired to entertain them after dinner. Wealthy women with time to spare read, wrote or listened to poetry, painted, embroidered, or played musical instruments. Family pets included dogs and caged birds.

Children were often taught dancing and music. They sang, and played whistles, pipes, or the cithara – a stringed instrument like a lyre.

▽ **Two gladiators in combat** shown on a vase from Colchester, Essex. The Romans introduced gladiator fighting to Britain as entertainment in about AD 100.

HOME IMPROVEMENTS

From time to time, owners altered their villas. They put on extensions, added new bathrooms, redecorated, and even changed the floor design. Everyone wanted the latest luxuries, especially new baths and heating systems.

▽ **Roman baths** had a wood-burning furnace to heat the rooms and water. The furnace was kept alight by slaves as long as the family was at home.

◁ **Remains of the Great Bath** at Bath in Avon. Water for the bath complex was piped from a Roman reservoir filled by a natural warm-water spring. Waste water and sewage was piped away into a nearby river.

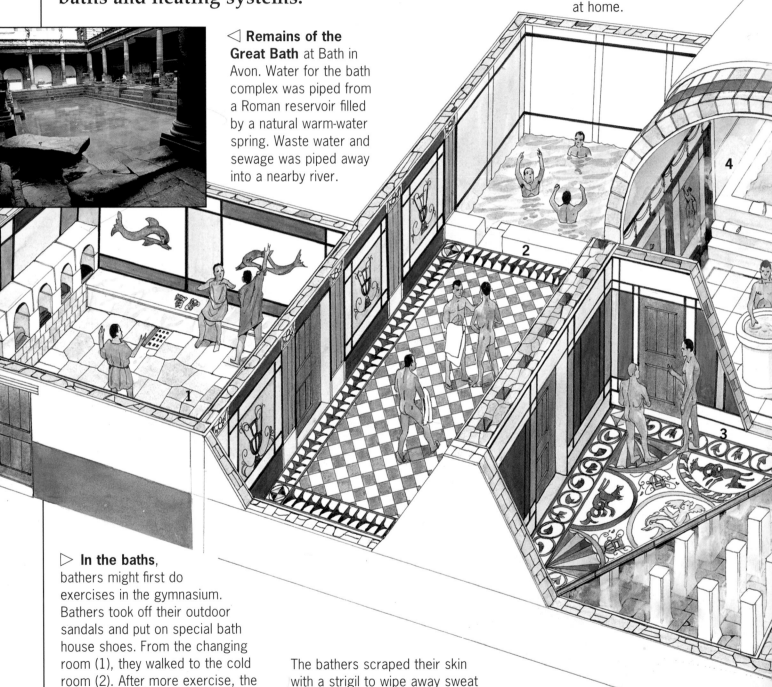

▷ **In the baths**, bathers might first do exercises in the gymnasium. Bathers took off their outdoor sandals and put on special bath house shoes. From the changing room (1), they walked to the cold room (2). After more exercise, the bathers went into the warm room (3) and next to the hot room (4).

The bathers scraped their skin with a strigil to wipe away sweat and dirt. After a hot splash came a massage with oils and a cold plunge.

◁ Remains of a hypocaust system at Fishbourne. The pillars in the centre would have supported the floor of a room, which has long since disappeared. Warm air passed along the stone and brick channels.

▷ A bronze strigil for scraping clean the skin, found at Bath.

Many villas were enlarged or improved in the 4th century. Chedworth, already large, had a big new dining room and two sets of baths – hot and cold – put in. In the 2nd century, fewer than ten British villas had mosaic floors. Two hundred years later, even modest villas had them. At this time, many villas were also replastered and freshly painted.

Some villas were enlarged to house a growing family. Chedworth may have been three separate houses later merged into one. New building was sometimes needed after a fire, or because wood and plaster decayed, or because the floor had sunk into soft earth. Mosaic floors also wore out with use. At Fishbourne, a floor built over a rubbish pit collapsed and needed relaying. Some of the old mosaic squares were kept for reuse while stone, cement and plaster rubble was spread over the old floor. Then thick cement was laid and a new mosaic set down.

When the floor was up, some owners put an under-floor hypocaust in a room heated only by a fire in a brazier. Strangely, several of these new baths and hypocausts were never used. Perhaps the villa owners spent all their money on improvements and could not afford to run them, or left Britain before they could be used and went to live in another part of the empire.

A DINNER PARTY

Dining in Roman times could be a very grand and expensive affair. Romans enjoyed dinner parties at their villas and liked to show off their wealth in a display of lavish hospitality.

Villas had a plentiful supply of fresh food from the farm and game from the woods. At the end of each day the family gathered for dinner in the large dining room. When the owner gave a dinner party, there were usually nine people present – three to a couch on each of three sides of a square. The fourth side was left empty for serving the meal. Diners lay propped on their left arms, using the right hand to pick up their food and drink. Guests brought their own napkins and knives.

At formal banquets, the host tried his best to surprise and please his guests. The Emperor Nero, at his palace in Rome, had dining rooms with spectacular effects – there was a revolving ceiling, and ivory panels that slid back to shower flowers or sprinkle perfume on to the diners.

State banquets in Britain could also be magnificent. The Emperor Hadrian visited the province in AD 122 and was probably entertained at the Governor's London palace. The two men may have discussed the emperor's plan to build a wall in the north of Britain, while they strolled before dinner in the gardens overlooking the River Thames.

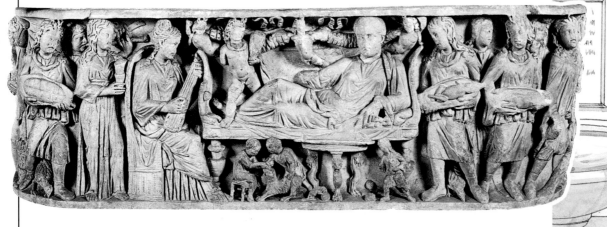

△ **Roman relief (scene cut in stone) from Italy** showing a feast in progress. The villa owner awaits his meal, resting on a dining couch. His wife sits in an armchair by his side, playing a stringed musical instrument. On either side, slaves bring dishes of meat, bread and vegetables, as well as pots of wine. The owner's children play at his feet with a pet dog. A mouse feeds on left-overs.

A Roman banquet had several courses, starting with a simple dish such as eggs, olives and lettuce. Then the servants would bring in dishes that startled the eye as well as filled the stomach – a pig roasted whole and stuffed with small birds, for example. Meat was often flavoured with a fish sauce.

△ **Palaces and great houses had rich treasures** that were usually kept out of sight for safekeeping. But on important occasions, all the gold and silver plate was on display. This great silver dish, 60 centimetres across, was found at Mildenhall in Suffolk but came from the Mediterranean area. It had been hidden with other riches in the 4th century when Britain was under threat from Saxon invaders.

◁ **Formal meals took a long time.** The host would invite his guests to stroll in the garden, for a breath of air between courses. While the diners chatted, the slaves cleared away empty plates and prepared for the next part of the banquet.

RUINS REMAINING

What we know of the great houses and villas of Roman Britain comes from clues found in the ground. These may be discovered while farmland is ploughed, or while foundations are dug for new buildings or roads.

▽ **How a Roman villa is revealed by archaeology.**
1. The ground plan is uncovered by digging.

Holes and foundations show where posts and walls once stood.
2. Evidence reveals how the early building looked.

3. From studying the outline and ruins, it is possible to construct the villa as it was in later Roman times.

△ **Outline of a villa.**

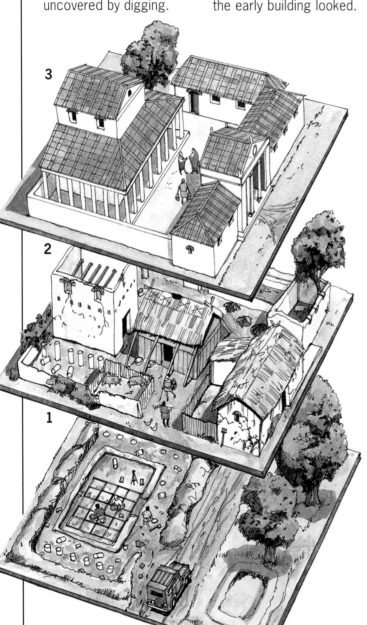

There are no Roman villas standing in Britain today. The buildings gradually decayed after the Roman army left Britain in AD 406. With no soldiers to sell produce to – and without Roman building skills or trade with the rest of the empire – the villa way of life ended.

However, stones from Roman houses survive where people reused them in later buildings. Lands that were part of villa estates are still used as farms today.

Remains of the Governor's London palace were found by archaeologists who knew what they were looking for. The remains of Roman country villas are often found by accident. Some, including Fishbourne and Chedworth villas, can still be seen by visitors today.

▽ **Remains of the Roman city walls at Silchester** can be seen in the foreground on the left of this aerial photograph. In the centre is the outline of a villa.

GLOSSARY

archaeology the study of history through objects left behind by earlier peoples.

audience chamber room where an important person receives visitors.

bow-drill string and bent wooden bow used to twist a point for making holes.

brazier moveable metal basket for holding a fire.

colonnades rows of columns holding up a roof over a walkway.

craftsmen people with a special skill or trade.

cult a system of religious belief.

excavation digging to reveal what lies underground.

frieze decorative edging of the wall of a room.

gladiators trained fighters who fought in front of an audience.

hypocaust underfloor space for heating by hot air.

magistrate official involved in settling matters of law.

mansion large house.

mason builder or stoneworker.

mosaic pattern made from small square cubes of coloured stone or glass.

overseer person who organizes or is in charge of work on an estate.

papyrus writing material made from plants.

parchment writing material made from animal skins.

scribes people employed to write.

seal official stamp.

shrine holy place where prayers and offerings are made.

stylus pointed instrument or pen for writing on wax tablets.

taxes money collected by a government.

threshing beating corn to separate grain from stalk.

veranda roofed platform around a house.

villa usually a house and outbuildings on a farm or estate, but also a large country house or palace.

▷ **Roman Britain.** This map shows the more important places mentioned in this book, including the Places to Visit listed on page 2.

TIMECHART

AD

43 The Romans invade Britain and begin their conquest. The army builds a supply depot at Fishbourne.

50 By this time the Romans are building London (Londinium) into a busy port-town, with a bridge across the Thames.

60 Revolt led by Boudicca.

60s-70s Villa at Fishbourne built.

75 First use of mosaic for floors in Britain around now.

84 Romans defeat Scottish tribes. Southern Britain at peace under Roman rule.

100 By now, London is the capital of Roman Britain.

122 Emperor Hadrian visits Britain. Work starts on building Hadrian's Wall.

150 New towns spur growth of villas to supply markets with produce.

197 Britain is divided into two provinces.

212 Emperor grants Roman citizenship to Britons.

200s Roman Britain at peace. Villas and towns built.

240 Temple of Mithras in London built about this date.

270 Fishbourne was not lived in after this date.

300 By now, some people in Roman Britain were Christians.

300s After a fire, the house at Fishbourne was demolished.

375 No new villas were built after this date.

400 Fire destroys Lullingstone villa.

410 British towns and villa-estates left to defend themselves from attacks by foreign invaders as Roman Empire weakens.

23

INDEX